What
Works

An Introductory Teacher Guide for Early Language and Emergent Literacy Instruction

Based on the National Early
Literacy Panel Report

familieslearning.org

Second Edition, Published February 2017

ISBN: 978-0-9987116-1-4

TABLE OF CONTENTS

About the National Center for Families Learning

NCFL's mission is to address our nation's literacy challenges by engaging all family members in learning, with a primary focus on parents and children living in poverty.

NCFL views education as a family affair. We see every parent as an asset; every family as a resource. By working together, we help families create their own learning networks. Whether it is obtaining a GED® credential, reading on grade level, or pursuing higher education, the results pave the way for economic self-sufficiency and propel families toward achieving their dreams, and our country toward collective success. Since 1991, more than 2 million families in more than 100 communities across the country have been impacted by programs developed by NCFL - our team has pioneered the concept of families learning and serving together to raise literacy levels and improve communities.

Vision and Mission

NCFL envisions a world in which all families are provided opportunities to improve their lives and become strong contributors to society. We address our nation's literacy challenges by engaging all family members in learning, with a primary focus on parents and children living in poverty.

Who We Serve

NCFL's tools and services can benefit all families. Our primary focus is to empower parents and children living in poverty and struggling with low literacy and language skills to improve their lives and become strong contributors to society.

What We Do

NCFL advances literacy and education by developing, implementing, and documenting innovative and promising two-generation practices, networks, and learning tools.

Our Partners

We lead and work with learners, administrators, teachers, librarians, policymakers, philanthropists, and advocates.

Visit NCFL at www.familieslearning.org

The Early Literacy Initiative is a project developed and implemented by the National Center for Families Learning (NCFL) with generous support from the Dollar General Literacy Foundation. This teacher guide is among several new and exciting early literacy products created through this partnership.

Through this initiative, NCFL is creating and disseminating a series of practical products for teachers and parents of children from birth through age five. These products are transforming the essential findings of the National Early Literacy Panel (NELP) into improved literacy instruction and support for our nation's preschool children. Laura Westberg, then Director of Special Projects and Research at NCFL directed the work of the NELP. The National Early Literacy Panel report was published in 2008.

The NELP panel included the following experts in literacy and early childhood education:

     Anne Cunningham, University of California, Berkeley

     Kathy Escamilla, University of Colorado at Boulder

     Janet Fischel, State University of New York at Stony Brook

     Susan H. Landry, University of Texas–Houston

     Christopher J. Lonigan, Florida State University

Victoria Molfese, University of Louisville
Chris Schatschneider, Florida State University
Timothy Shanahan, NELP chair, University of Illinois at Chicago
Dorothy Strickland, Rutgers University

NCFL recognizes the work of the guide's authors, Donna Bell and Laura Westberg; copy editor, Gail Price; and communications specialist, Meg Ivey. This guide was enhanced by the constructive feedback and valuable suggestions of the internal and external expert reviewers.

Other early literacy products can be found at NCFL's Web site, http://www.familieslearning.org.

The purpose of this guide is to help teachers understand the research reported in *Developing Early Literacy: Report of the National Early Literacy Panel* (NELP, 2008). The guide describes ways teachers can use the research effectively for early childhood instruction, assessment, choosing curriculum, and helping parents better support their young children's language and literacy learning. Based on the evidence reported by the National Early Literacy Panel (NELP), this guide will help teachers and program administrators make a significant difference in young children's literacy learning. It is not enough to base instructional decisions on what we "think" or "feel" is effective. Armed with findings from this report, instructional decisions now can be based on what is *known* to improve early language and literacy learning. Programs that have a literacy-focused preschool curriculum are going to realize far better outcomes for children than those that do not have such a curriculum. This may mean investing in professional development because teachers who are trained to provide instruction based on research-proven information will get far better outcomes.

The National Early Literacy Panel Report

The NELP Report identifies the converging evidence about building children's language and literacy skills in the preschool period. It identifies the early skills that give children the strongest foundation for learning to read, spell, and write. It can be used to inform decisions about development of, and selecting, the most appropriate curriculum for use in early childhood classrooms (e.g., decisions about the content, the intensity, and sequence of instruction). It can serve as a guide for preservice and inservice professional development of both new and practicing early childhood educators, not only in identifying the focus for early literacy instruction, but also in adopting practices proven to be more effective in supporting young children's language and literacy learning.

The National Early Literacy Panel was composed of nine nationally-known researchers who brought a rich and diverse record of research in the areas of reading, early literacy and language, cognition, English as a second language, pediatrics, special education, research methodology, and early childhood education to the completion of a **research synthesis** on early language and literacy development. The panel was convened to conduct a synthesis – a review, analysis, and summary – of data gathered from qualified research studies of early literacy skills and interventions in children ages birth to five. The panel

Research synthesis: a study that objectively and systematically collects, analyzes, and evaluates data from pre-existing studies to determine answers to specified research questions

used strict criteria for the types of studies that could be included. The resulting report is intended to contribute to decisions in educational policy and practice that affect early literacy development and to determine best ways for teachers and families to support young children's language and literacy development.

The receptive literacy skills of decoding and reading comprehension and the expressive literacy skills of spelling and writing are widely recognized as

Conventional literacy skills: the abilities of decoding, reading comprehension, spelling, and writing

conventional literacy skills and abilities. However, these skills are not typically evidenced in the early childhood years because preschool children are not reading and writing in conventional ways. Therefore, the NELP first needed to identify the early and emerging literacy skills and abilities of children birth through five years that *are related to and predict* these later conventional literacy skills.

The NELP found that six early language and literacy skills are moderately to strongly linked to later conventional literacy outcomes: *alphabet knowledge, phonological awareness, rapid naming of letters and digits, rapid naming of objects and colors, writing or writing name,* and *phonological short term memory.* The panel found five other important skills – *concepts about print, print knowledge, reading readiness, oral language,* and *visual processing* – that correlated moderately with at least one conventional literacy skill. Areas with a smaller effect or with substantially weaker relationships and that were examined in fewer studies or with fewer children included *visual skills* (such as visual motor, visual memory skills, and visual perceptual skills) and *environmental print* (such as the ability to decode or read common signs and logos).

Early literacy skills linked to later conventional literacy outcomes:
- Alphabet knowledge
- Phonological awareness
- Rapid naming of letters and digits
- Rapid naming of objects and colors
- Writing or writing name
- Phonological short term memory
- Concepts about print
- Print knowledge
- Reading readiness
- Oral language
- Visual processing
- Visual skills
- Environmental print

Once these early literacy skills were identified, the panel analyzed the types of methods, strategies, programs, and instructional practices (**interventions**) used with young children that support or inhibit these early and emerging literacy skills for

Interventions:
the instructional practices, methods, strategies, approaches, and programs used by educators and parents to mediate learning

children within the ages of birth to 5 (including kindergarten). What are the interventions that support the development of these skills? How can this knowledge inform what all early childhood teachers should do in order to better support children's success in learning conventional literacy skills?

The Goal for Language and Literacy Instruction

Literacy is only one part of early childhood development, but often it is the barometer for the other areas of development. The goal for language and literacy instruction is for teachers to integrate early literacy skills into instructional approaches that are appropriate and engaging for young children, and that are explicit and intensive enough to offer a strong foundation for children's later reading success. Although these skills individually are important in leading to positive conventional literacy outcomes, *a combination of them provides the greatest success to later reading and writing.*

It is also important to note that the panel examined whether or not particular circumstances made interventions more or less effective. For example, did the interventions work better in particular settings or environments, such as a preschool program or at home? Were results better in rural or urban settings? Additionally, did characteristics of children influence the effectiveness of the interventions? Did they work better with children who are disadvantaged or in poverty versus children who are not? Were some interventions more effective for younger children than for older children?

The NELP found few demographic differences in children's learning patterns. The interventions worked equally well across all economic levels, ethnicities, and population density (e.g., urban, suburban, rural settings, or a combination of these). Providing age-appropriate interventions for young children is a common idea for early childhood classrooms. However, there were few important differences among the studies with regard to age or developmental level. For the most part, when age or developmental level comparisons were possible, effects were obtained with groups of both younger and older children. The results for children who had prior literacy knowledge (such as knowing their letters) were similar to those who did not have that prior knowledge. Interventions were equally effective for children at-risk and not at-risk, and for children with and without special needs. Most instructional strategies effective in kindergarten are similar to those used in preschool.

Although evidence exists showing that many early literacy skills have moderate to strong relationships with later conventional literacy skills (see *early literacy skills* box on the previous page), there is no evidence to indicate these skills should become targets of instruction

Many of these findings might fall under the research adage, "correlation does not imply causation." Inherently, there are many reasons that two variables may be related, but only one of these reasons is that one skill "causes" the other.

Consequently, effective use of the NELP findings requires combining both the predictor results and the intervention results to identify those skills that are precursors to conventional literacy skills and for which there is evidence for effective instructional practice and causal relationships. These skills, as determined by the NELP, are *alphabet knowledge*, *phonological awareness* and *oral language.*

Precursor skills with instructional evidence:
- Alphabet knowledge
- Phonological awareness
- Oral language

The National Center for Families Learning (NCFL) believes strongly, as a result of their work with the NELP, that the panel's findings have tremendous potential to improve future reading achievement by influencing the literacy learning of young children. For this reason, NCFL has distilled the research findings into this practical and useful guide for early literacy practitioners.

Assessing Children's Early Language and Literacy Learning

Assessment and accountability are expected elements of educational programs. Early childhood educators are interested in monitoring children's progress and in identifying children who need targeted intervention to promote early literacy skills. They use assessments that provide reliable and valid measurements of these skills. The NELP findings suggest that instruction focused on early literacy skills may provide valuable literacy preparation, particularly for children at risk for developing reading difficulties. These findings provide guidance to early childhood educators for selecting appropriate curricula for the children they serve. They also provide guidance to curriculum developers concerning the skills that should be targeted within instructional activities. To determine if instruction is making a difference for young children, it is vital that progress is monitored over time in a systematic way. Assessing children's attainment of essential skills allows teachers to target instruction to individual children and to modify their instruction in ways that have the most benefit for the majority of children.

Both formal and informal assessments can be appropriate and useful in evaluating individual students, as well as in evaluating aspects of instruction and curriculum.

Many teachers *informally assess* children's educational progress by observing and reflecting on their participation during instruction and play. This informal snapshot can indicate areas of strength, skills that may need additional support and reinforcement, misunderstandings to clarify, or places where children are or are not ready to progress to another skill area or level. Because these informal assessments are based on teacher perceptions and observations they are most beneficial when considered cumulatively – where similar behaviors have been observed in a variety of situations over time. Instructional decisions are strengthened, however, when based on both informal and formal assessment.

Formal assessment provides a systematic approach to screen, test, monitor progress, and document child outcomes. Assessments not only provide reliable and valid measurements of children's early literacy skills, but also provide essential information for guiding instruction. The selection of a particular assessment tool should be intentional. After selection, methods for documenting results, and a plan for communicating results to parents and other professionals should be identified. If appropriate, the screening or assessment should be administered two to three times a year by trained staff.

Teachers informally monitor progress of children's language and literacy skill development by:

- Recording specific observations of children's use of language and literacy skills in meaningful interactions
- Collecting and examining children's language and literacy work samples
- Using curriculum-based assessments
- Using language- and literacy-based checklists or rating scales

Both informal and formal assessments of student learning can be helpful in making decisions about how to engage young children in ways that increase their language and literacy development. If gaps or deficits are identified, improvements can be made. This might indicate a need for changes in curriculum and instructional practices, improved teacher skills, or a focused professional development plan.

Using This Guide

It is important to know which particular programs or forms of instruction bring about the desired early literacy outcomes in children, or actually produce the desired outcomes in conventional literacy. Therefore, presenting and describing the instructional methods of the various interventions leading to these outcomes is the central focus of this teacher's guide.

In general, the NELP found that a wide range of interventions had positive impacts on children's early literacy learning. These positive results were due to the nature and intensity of the instructional activities examined in the studies. For these interventions, especially the ones that involved high-impact instructional strategies, the activities and procedures were different from those typically seen in early childhood classrooms. For instance, in many cases researchers or their agents delivered many of the interventions. In addition, the majority of the interventions across the categories were either delivered as one-on-one or small group activities, occurred frequently, and were adult directed. These findings provide information for teachers on how to organize instruction with young children by focusing on more effective small group and one-on-one instruction. Teachers can be more intentional about how literacy interactions are planned and implemented by thoughtfully following large group instructional activities with small group or individualized instruction to maximize benefits.

Three categories of interventions that both measured the strong to moderate early literacy skills and showed evidence for effective instruction are:

1. Code-focused interventions
2. Oral language interventions
3. Shared reading interventions

After identifying the interventions that supported or inhibited skills leading to conventional literacy outcomes, the panel investigated whether the environment or setting where the intervention took place (such as a home, Head Start, Even Start, or Montessori program) impacted later outcomes in reading, writing, or spelling; and whether there were particular characteristics in children (such as special needs, poverty, or a particular age) that were linked to the later outcomes in reading, writing, or spelling. These were important considerations because they might influence recommendations for practices of early childhood educators and parents in supporting young children's language and literacy learning.

Each section of the guide describes one of the three intervention types and includes:

- Relevant skills and evidence-based instruction
- Findings from the NELP Report
- Examples of instruction
- Simple ways of assessing children's progress
- Recommended resources for further exploration

In addition to looking at valid instructional practices within these three types of interventions, this guide also includes sections that describe:

- Parents' positive influence on their children's early literacy skills as a result of parent and home program interventions examined by the NELP
- Print awareness and early writing as predictors of early reading
- Teacher planning for literacy-focused instruction

This guide presents the skills and instructional approaches that were found to have the greatest effect on improving children's language and literacy development. It is an introduction to the results of the NELP Report and gives a basic beginning for putting the findings into practice. It is not intended to serve as a literacy curriculum or program for implementing language and literacy instruction. However, the content certainly can be used to guide the selection of a curriculum and the types of instructional choices and practices made regularly in early childhood classrooms; to suggest the use of assessment as an important tool for informing instruction; to make decisions about professional development needs; and to influence the types of information and support provided for the parents of children served in early childhood programs. There are areas of early language and literacy development that have not been adequately researched – the NELP Report only reflects information about what is currently known relative to what has been studied.

What Is Code-Focused Instruction?

Code-focused instruction helps children learn the alphabetic principle – the knowledge that letters in written words represent sounds in spoken words. The process of learning to read involves "cracking" this code in order to translate these printed symbols into words.

What Are the Key Findings Regarding Code-Focused Instruction?

A body of research indicates that early, systematic, explicit phonemic awareness instruction can successfully jump-start emergent and early readers' reading performance" (McGee & Ukrainetz, 2009). Code-focused skills are important early literacy skills that predict conventional literacy skills, specifically outcomes for decoding, spelling and reading comprehension. Code-focused skills include the ability to know and manipulate the sounds within spoken words (phonological awareness), and to know the letters of the alphabet and combine the letters with the sounds they represent (alphabet knowledge). Code-focused skills also include early decoding abilities in ways that later help with decoding print. Code-focused instruction for preschool and kindergarten children targets these areas.

Code-focused skills: the abilities of phonological awareness, alphabet knowledge, and early decoding or phonics

What are the best ways to teach code-focused skills? According to the NELP, teaching phonological awareness alone provides positive results.

Teaching phonological awareness as well as alphabet knowledge revealed better results, and teaching phonological awareness skills with phonics or early decoding achieves the strongest outcomes for children. Thus, instruction can be more effective when a number of skills are combined.

Because code-focused skills are related so strongly to learning to read and spell successfully, it is important that preschool educators use related instructional strategies to promote skill development. Whether children are in preschool or kindergarten, focusing instruction on phonological awareness skills can have a significant effect on children's literacy learning. This is particularly important for teachers working with children considered to be at risk for reading difficulties, because most children who have difficulty reading have problems with code-focused skills. Effective code-focused instruction can and should be provided in the context of a developmentally appropriate early childhood classroom that includes direct instruction as well as play and discovery learning.

Code-focused instruction needs to be systematic, explicit, and intentional and needs to include many opportunities for practice. Providing code-focused instruction only within incidental opportunities that may (or may not) arise means that children are most likely not receiving adequate instruction within this important area. Children need to be told explicitly what they are doing and understand that these are important skills to have in order to become successful readers. Teachers need to plan what skills they are going to teach to which group of students, the pace at which the instruction is provided, and if the skills will be taught one-on-one, in small groups or to the whole class.

Overall recommendations for code-focused instruction are to:
- Include instruction where children are taught one-on-one or in small homogeneous groups. Current research did not include any studies identifying whether or not large group code-focused instruction with preschoolers is effective.
- Model the pronunciation of words clearly, without distortion and without raising or lowering the voice in a "sing-song" fashion.

- Model the spacing between sounds when doing blending and segmenting activities. For instance, in segmenting syllables, be careful not to repeat letter consonant sounds in words that contain repeated consonants such as *letter* (*le/ter*, not *let/ter*).
- Have children focus on the sound structure of the new words as well as the meaning. For example, explain both the meaning of the word *cowboy* while helping children recognize that this compound word is actually made of two smaller familiar words.

Phonological Awareness Instruction

Phonological awareness is the ability to hear and manipulate the separate sounds within words independent of the words' meanings. This ability is directly linked to later reading ability, making this a vital area of instruction for preschool educators. Being able to hear the separate sounds in words gives children an ability to "sound out" unfamiliar words when reading as well as to connect the separate sounds to letters for spelling. However, this can be especially difficult because individual sounds in words are co-articulated with the other sounds surrounding them when pronounced (e.g., the /b/ in *beet* versus *bought*). Children must be able to hear and identify the distinct sounds of the individual phonemes when words are pronounced even though the sounds that make up the word are co-articulated.

Phonological awareness: the ability to hear and manipulate the separate sounds within words

Direct code-focused instruction needs to consider both the cognitive operation and the complexity of the language skills being taught – the size of sound units children are manipulating and in what way they are manipulating them.

1. **Level of linguistic complexity** of sound units being taught ranges on a continuum from larger units, such as words to smaller and smaller units, such as syllables, onsets/rimes, and phonemes.

2. **Cognitive operation** is the task children are performing on sound units, such as identifying sounds, blending sounds, or deleting sounds.

Linguistic complexity: the size of sound units which children are taught

Cognitive operation: the learning task children are performing on sound units

Development of phonological awareness skills follows a progression from large to small – from whole words to smaller and smaller units of sound. Children first learn to use whole words in phrases and sentences. Next they learn to manipulate the smaller parts within words, such as breaking apart compound words (*bathtub* = *bath* + *tub*) and syllables (*candy* = /*can*/ + /*dy*/). A syllable is a unit of sound that has one vowel sound. Each syllable has one and only one vowel sound, regardless of how many actual vowels appear in the syllable. Then children learn to distinguish the beginning consonant sound in syllables (the **onset**) and separate that from the vowel and the rest of the syllable (the **rime**), e.g., *dog* = /*d*/ + /*og*/. Finally they are able to hear and manipulate the smallest parts within spoken words (phonemes), e.g., *cat* = /*k*/ + /*a*/ + /*t*/. Keep in mind that children do not have to master each skill before progressing to the next. Many of these skills may develop at the same time. Teaching phonological awareness achieves results across all emergent literacy skills and conventional literacy skills.

Onset:
the beginning consonant sound in a syllable

Rime:
the vowel and all that follows it in the syllable

Examples of activities that teach phonological awareness where children manipulate sounds in words:

- **Identity** tasks – children identify words, such as "which two words begin with the same sound?"
- **Synthesis** activities (which are considered more challenging than identity tasks and easier than analysis tasks) include:

  * Blend syllables to make words (/*pen*/ + /*cil*/)
  * Blend phonemes to make words (/*m*/ + /*a*/ + /*p*/)

Synthesis:
putting together as in blending

Analysis:
breaking or taking apart

- **Analysis** tasks (which are usually more difficult than identity and synthesis tasks and get better results once children can perform them) include:

  * Breaking a word into syllables, such as *basket* = /*bas*/ + /*ket*/

  * Deleting sounds, such as deleting the /*k*/ sound in *clip* leaves *lip*

* Producing words and sounds is more difficult than recognizing the sounds within spoken words. Tasks that ask children to make a choice (which one of these words…?) are often easier for children than tasks where they have to think up words on their own (say a word that sounds like…)

* Using nonverbal cues and/or visual props is helpful for encouraging responses and sustaining children's attention. An example of a nonverbal cue is to hold your hand up as a signal for children to listen while you are saying a word, and then drop your hand when it is time for them to respond. Clapping out words or syllables in words is another example of a nonverbal cue. Teachers use visual props when they hold apart pictures of two separate words and then move them together as the compound word is created. In addition, pictures can be cut into the same number of puzzle pieces as the number of syllables in the word being depicted, such as a three-part puzzle for the word *gorilla.* Counters can be used one-to-one for matching the syllables or sounds in a word.

* Make activities more challenging when children are ready to move into more difficult tasks. You might provide more choices when looking at pictures of things beginning with the same sound. Another example for making a task more challenging is to make word choices more similar, requiring careful discrimination. When given three word choices, it is easier to tell which two words begin with the same sound when the words share only one sound (as the /b/ in *cat, bird, bell*). It is more difficult if the word choices share other sounds as well (*cat, bat, bird: bat* and *bird* share the /b/ sound, but children may be confused by the shared /–at/ sound in *cat* and *bat*).

* Rhyming activities have long been a staple of many early childhood classrooms. However, asking children to produce words that rhyme is an advanced activity requiring higher level skills that are typical of older children. Research has shown that children make less progress when instruction focuses primarily on rhyming activities rather than on other types of phonological awareness activities. This does not mean we don't continue to include rhymes, rhyming books and songs in our early childhood classrooms. These are playful, fun language activities that children enjoy and they may help children attend to sounds in words. However, rhyming activities are not sufficient and they should not

replace other more effective forms of phonological awareness instruction.

* Because children within a preschool classroom will be at various skill levels of phonological awareness, teachers need to assess children to identify the range of instruction that matches each child's abilities. After a formal or informal assessment, teachers can place children in small groups based on their need for similar types of instructional focus. As children learn new skills, these groups can be reorganized in order to best match learners to types of instructional activities.

Phonological Awareness Instruction Paired with Alphabet Knowledge

Letter knowledge skills "facilitate the acquisition of decoding ability and can be taught effectively with preschool children" (Phillips, Clancy-Menchetti & Lonigan, 2008, p. 12). Almost all of the studies included in the code-focused intervention category of the NELP Report indicated that teaching phonological awareness strategies while also teaching children the letters of the alphabet had a larger impact on children's literacy development than teaching either of these alone. However, children must first know enough about letters to be able to benefit from pairing the instruction for these skills. Teachers may need to use formal and informal assessment to determine whether or not children have letter knowledge to be able to integrate letter instruction with phonological awareness instruction. All of the tasks for teaching phonological awareness also apply to teaching letter-names and letter-sounds including the importance of systematic and explicit instruction.

Alphabet knowledge is the recognition of letters as distinct symbols that have specific names and specific sounds associated with them and is a strong predictor of later reading success. Along with the phonological activities described above, children also can be learning specific aspects about print, such as letter-names and letter-sounds because both are strong predictors of decoding skill and each supports learning in the other. There are many programs for teaching letter-names and letter-sounds, but little evidence that evaluates and compares these program choices. It does appear that "children may benefit from learning letter-

Alphabet knowledge: the recognition of letters as distinct symbols that have specific names and specific sounds associated with them

names before letter-sounds" (Justice, Pence, Bowles, & Wiggins, 2006; Share, 2004, as cited in Phillips et al., 2008, p. 13). However, teachers should focus on providing many opportunities for all children to learn all the letter names and as many sounds as possible, planning for exposure and instructional opportunities where children can manipulate and practice using letters. Children typically are most interested in learning the letters in their own names, and often these are the first letters taught.

Following are examples of types of activities that should be included for teaching alphabet knowledge. Think about incorporating these kinds of things into other routines and activities within your classroom.

- Model the letter names and sounds for children to hear.
- Show a letter and ask the child to point out the same letter. "This is a *G* (or ask the child to name the letter). Look at these letters. Can you find another *G*?"
- Ask children to identify the name of a letter as you point to it.
- Ask children to discriminate between different letters ("Point to the letter *P*."). The greater number of letters shown, the more difficult this task will be.
- Use children's printed names in a variety of ways such as identifying helpers, choosing who will play in particular learning areas, and determining who is ready to line-up for outside play. For example, "Let's read these names: Gina, Gayla and George. How are they alike? That's right– they all begin with G. They can go outside with Ms. Lisa."
- Use print for signs in learning areas (Block, Play, Math Center, etc.), recipes for cooking activities (e.g., directions, using pictures and print, for making toast), menus for meals (Today's Lunch: milk, lasagna, pears), and to show where materials belong. For example, print the word *maracas* inside their outlined drawing to show where to hang them in the music area.

Phonological Awareness Instruction Paired with Phonics

When phonological awareness instruction is paired with phonics instruction, children show the greatest gains in their literacy development. **Phonics** instruction focuses on the relationship of the sounds in spoken words and their associated letters and groups of letters as they appear in print.

Phonics:
a method of instruction focused on teaching the relationship between the sounds in spoken words and their associated symbols in print

Once children know the letters of the alphabet and the associated letter-sounds, teachers can integrate phonological awareness and phonics instruction by incorporating letter and print skills into synthesis and analysis activities. For example, adapt these phonological awareness activities by including letters and print in the following ways:

- Identify onsets – Show three printed words, clearly read each word, and ask children to identify which words begin with the same sound. (*boy, girl, gate*).
- Blend syllables – Show the syllables, each printed on a card. Read them separately and move the cards together, asking children to say the word made when the syllables are blended (*/pen/ + /cil/*).
- Blend phonemes – Give each child a card with a letter printed on it and ask children to stand in the order in which the letters are used. Have children hold up the letter cards and move them closer and closer together as the letter-sounds are blended to read the word (*/m/ + /a/ + /p/*).
- Delete sounds – Show a card with a word printed on it, such as clip, and read the word aloud. As you cover the beginning sound, ask children to say the word that is made without the beginning sound (deleting the */k/* sound in *clip* makes *lip*).
- Change the onset – First review the sounds of various consonants by showing them and asking children to say the letter sound. Then show a printed word, such as *cat*, and read it. Ask children to say the word with you – *cat*. Cover the onset and ask children to say the word – *at*. Next cover the onset with one of the consonant letters, such as *b* and ask children to say the new word – *bat*.

Other Important Instructional Considerations for Phonological Awareness

Computer-assisted instruction has been identified as an effective way for supporting code-focused skill development (Hecht & Close, 2002; Mioduser, Tur-Kaspa & Leitner, 2000). Both hardware and software should be evaluated for accommodating abilities and interest levels of young children, such as the use of "high-quality digitized speech for instruction, song activities, and presentation of visual stimuli... colorful graphic displays that help motivate performances in a game-like setting." Instruction that includes a heavy concentration on phonological awareness skills can be integrated with activities focusing on letter knowledge, print concepts, and oral language skills (Hecht & Close, 2002, p. 100). Studies show that children exposed to CAI make significantly greater gains on rhyming skills, and their expressive vocabulary scores were predictive of pre- to posttest growth (Lonigan, et al., 2003).

When choosing computer-assisted programs for preschool children, consider:
- Instruction is interactive
- Can be done independent of teacher instruction
- Includes colorful animation and sound
- Provides a demonstration for children
- Provides children with feedback and support to correct

Effective code-focused instruction should move quickly enough to keep children attentive and engaged, resulting in on-task behavior and more time for practice. Following a fairly predictable lesson format and focusing on only one skill at a time, helps teachers and children focus more on the content, rather than on the process. Incorporate repetition and review into the lesson plans and into the long-term curriculum plan to help children master and revisit skills, concepts, and vocabulary.

Code-focused instruction should:

- Be provided individually, or in small groups of three to five children
- Happen consistently – daily, or two to three times each week
- Take place in sessions that last from 15 to 30 minutes, based on the needs and interests of the children
- Include both synthesis and analysis activities (most effective when integrated with alphabet knowledge)

- Become more challenging over time

Be explicit in explaining to students what you are asking them to do and provide examples of what the activity looks like when they do it. Below are suggested steps to follow when providing code-focused instruction.

1. *Define* the concept being taught. For example, explain that "compound words are words that are made when two separate words are combined to make a new, different word" (Phillips et al., 2008, p. 9).

2. Then *model* and *explain*. "When I put *base* and *ball* together, they become *baseball*."

3. Provide *guided practice*. The amount and type of practice provided depends on how much support the child needs to successfully perform the task. During practice, teachers observe and assess, and provide support, such as repeated demonstration using other examples, or more guided practice. It might mean the activity needs to be broken into simpler steps or that a visual or concrete example is needed. "Let's make some compound words together." Showing cards with pictures and the corresponding printed words that you gradually move together ask, "What compound word is made when we put together *cow* and *boy*?"

4. Give *feedback*. While children are first learning the new skill, give positive reinforcement immediately following the desired response to let them know what they are doing right. "Excellent! *Cowboy* is the compound word made by combining the smaller words *cow* and *boy*. What is a cowboy?" When giving a child corrective feedback, be sure to know if the error is due to lack of knowledge or lack of attention. If an error occurs because the child lacks understanding, additional instructional support is needed. If the error is due to lack of attention, the teacher needs to focus on minimizing distractions and boosting the child's motivation. Keep feedback positive so that "all children can feel successful, motivated, and supported regardless of their actual performance" (Phillips et al., 2008, p. 10).

5. Allow many opportunities for *independent practice* within direct instruction. Teachers are able to observe and informally assess individual children's skill levels in order to make good instructional decisions as to

whether a child needs additional support or is ready to try something more challenging. For example, using sets of cards, have children take turns combining smaller words to create compound words. These may be real compound words or nonsense words. *Stop* and *light* combine to make the compound word *stoplight*. You might ask, "What compound word is created when we combine *cow* and *stop – cowstop!* How might we describe a *cowstop?*"

In addition to opportunities for independent practice within regularly scheduled phonological awareness instruction, teachers can provide opportunities for children to use these skills throughout their school day, both within teacher-led and free-choice types of experiences. For example, children might connect two-part puzzles to create compound words; clap syllables as the class sings the words to a song; talk about the words that have the same onset when reading a story with alliteration; or use objects that begin with a particular sound in the dramatic play area. While there is no indication these more implicit activities have a positive effect, they are typically enjoyable and can certainly supplement explicit instructional strategies.

Summary

It is important to provide code-focused instruction to improve the emergent skills of phonological awareness and alphabet knowledge. This includes providing instruction that builds an ability to *hear* and *manipulate* the sounds in words (phonological awareness), know alphabet letters and the speech sounds they represent (alphabet knowledge), and to combine those skills in order to decode print. If early childhood teachers improve only one aspect of their teaching, it should be to increase both the quantity and quality of planned instruction devoted to code-focused learning. To get the best results, pair phonological instruction with phonics instruction. Because it is recommended that direct code-focused instruction be implemented one-on-one or in small groups, teachers can accommodate the range of skill levels within a classroom by assigning children to small developmental groups. This placement allows for flexibility as children advance along a continuum of skill acquisition.

To support the acquisition of code-focused skills, instruction needs to include complexity in the types of skills being taught and to address a variety of skills within the range of complexity. Different skills should be practiced at the same time. For example: during instruction focused on phonological awareness, children can do blending activities and synthesis activities such as breaking words into syllables. When teaching letter knowledge, teaching letter-names before letter-sounds is effective. Use nonverbal cues and visual props to facilitate instruction and sustain children's interest. Use informal and formal assessment for guiding instructional practices, to provide additional skills focus, and for informing small group assignments. Finally, regularly follow a plan that incorporates elements of good instruction, including defining what is being taught, modeling and explaining, providing guided practice with feedback, and opportunities for independent practice.

What Is Print Awareness?

Print awareness refers to tasks combining elements of alphabet knowledge, concepts about print, and early decoding. In most instances, the use of print dictates the conventions that are followed. For example, a list serves a specific purpose and looks different than a story; maps use print for labeling and also include a key or legend. Pictures can be described in many ways, but the words represented through print are the same words each time they are read.

> **Print awareness:** tasks combining elements of alphabet knowledge, concepts about print, and early decoding

Following the rules of grammar, stringing words together form sentences and a series of sentences can form stories, represent ideas and share information.

What Are the Key Findings Regarding Print Awareness?

The NELP found that print awareness strategies and techniques are used in shared reading approaches and some code-focused interventions, but rarely are there intervention studies that have solely tested print awareness as an isolated skill. In addition, programs that included both phonological awareness and a print-focused component had a stronger effect on print-specific outcomes, such as alphabet knowledge.

Supporting Print Awareness in the Classroom Environment

Exposure to the numerous uses of print is influenced by language and culture and can differ greatly for each child. Print experiences within the home and early childhood classroom can be planned by addressing the materials provided, the exposure and uses, and the interactions that occur between adults and children. Children must have many opportunities to experience the varied and meaningful uses of print (Strickland & Schickedanz, 2004, p. 21).

Examples of materials for children to access and use that support print awareness include: writing supplies such as various types of paper and writing instruments; magnetic letters and various letter manipulatives; alphabet books, charts, and cards; a variety of books and book genres; board games; manipulatives and activities to sort, match, and classify related to shapes and symbols. Children need experiences with painting, writing, and using a computer; reading and producing books; and with print used regularly in meaningful ways – charts with names, a daily schedule, message boards, and name and picture labels for storing materials and designating learning areas.

In an early childhood classroom environment, print, writing, and other literacy materials are part of every learning center. Children's names should be used in many ways, such as labeling cubbies and mailboxes, and designating helpers and groups. Foster an awareness of print by sharing information, such as the day's schedule, the alphabet, or reading the daily menu. Use print in the classroom in meaningful ways, by using helper charts, weather graphs, and science observations. Use print to solve problems including using recipes, and directions for games, maps, and phone directories. Children should be encouraged to write their own names upon arrival and on their art work. Provide name models for each child and have available throughout the classroom.

Place relevant books in all learning centers, along with writing utensils (markers, pencils, paper, notepads, clipboards, cards, chalk, white boards and markers, and more…) in order to facilitate both reading and writing, and the acknowledgement of print for these purposes, with children all day long and throughout the early childhood environment.

Finally, show how using message boards, notes, letters, and newsletters to families are valuable for communicating with others. Make available and use books, newspapers, magazines, postings of favorite songs, poems, and rhymes for fun. As children learn letter names, adults use informal activities and games for supporting letter-sound correspondence such as "I spy something that begins with ___" or "Stand up if your name begins with ___"

To support the development of print awareness, adults should: model meaningful uses of print; include print as an important element throughout the classroom setting; incorporate print into play and instructional activities in planned and purposeful ways that support each child's skill level and scaffolds learning; provide encouragement, guidance, and praise as children use print.

Incorporating Print Awareness into Activities and Daily Routines

There are a number of ways to incorporate print awareness into children's activities and daily routines.

Remember, the effectiveness of phonological awareness instruction is enhanced when it incorporates a print focus, as described earlier in examples of instruction that incorporate alphabet knowledge (see Code-Focused Instruction, page 13). Book reading provides a natural opportunity for modeling the uses and characteristics of print, and the interactive nature of shared reading is ideal for facilitating print awareness instruction in explicit ways. During book reading, look at the cover and point to the title, and the author's and illustrator's names, while reading the words to build book knowledge. Point to words and to specific letters that have special relevance for children, such as the first letter of a child's name. Point to a specific word or phrase that is repeated, or used as a refrain in a story, and encourage children to identify that word or phrase elsewhere as you read.

As children grow in their understanding of print, incorporate information about the conventions and characteristics of print, such as directionality, spacing, punctuation, organization, and the use of upper- and lower-case letters, into instruction. For example, help children understand the importance of space around words by having them point to one word on a page, find the first word on the page, or to count the number of words on a page.

There are many occasions for observing children's awareness of print and early writing skills when you provide an environment rich with opportunities for children to use print.

Look for:

- Children's interest in knowing what printed words say and in writing and signing their own names
- Interest and involvement in using print during instructional activities
- An increase in the number of letters recognized and known
- Integration of print use and writing into play activities
- Progress over time in learning the conventions and characteristics associated with print

Summary

Having an awareness of the basic elements and constructs of print is an important strand woven into the fabric of learning to read and write. It advances children's learning of the alphabetic principle. It includes an understanding that there are many different and useful purposes for print, which enhance our ability to understand and do many things. This broad range of uses also means that print takes on many different forms. Books, signs, letters, envelopes, lists, recipes, receipts, instructions, and maps each has a typical structure that matches its purpose and facilitates its use. Provide these types of age-appropriate items in the classroom for children to use and explore, during their work and play. Print in the early childhood classroom should be purposeful and provided with intent.

Print awareness is supported through provision of a print-rich learning environment that allows children to see and experience the many uses and forms of print. This indirect approach for supporting print awareness, while intentional and planned, should be combined with code-focused and shared reading instruction.

Early childhood teachers can provide meaningful activities that address the basic conventions and characteristics of print, starting with some of the most basic elements of written language. Children must learn letter-names and letter-sounds and print directionality. They must learn that words are formed by an intentional arrangement of letters and that the white space separates words; that together words create sentences and are used collectively to tell a story or relay information. Teachers support these skills when they point to individual letters, words, and elements of print when reading aloud. They explain elements specific to different types of print, the uses and different formats followed for each. They also provide opportunities for children to write and practice their own developing knowledge and skills.

What Is Oral Language?

Oral language refers to the ability to produce and comprehend spoken language (NELP, 2008, p. 43). It is a broad construct consisting of a variety of discrete language skills such as **expressive** and **receptive vocabulary**, **grammar**, **definitional vocabulary**, **syntax**, and **listening comprehension**. The skills associated with speaking and listening include the ability to understand the meaning and use of appropriate words and to group them into phrases and sentences following standard organizational rules (grammar) that communicate a message that others can understand. We use words to express ourselves as well as to understand others. "The importance of language to an individual's success cannot be overstated" (Benner, et al., 2002, p. 67).

What Are the Key Findings Regarding Oral Language?

The strongest relationship oral language development has with later decoding and reading comprehension is to teach a composite of oral language skills (combining these skills together), rather than a single skill at a time. Although the NELP found oral language to be a weak predictor of later conventional literacy skills by itself, when an instructional focus combines the teaching of many oral language skills together, children make gains.

The NELP wanted to look more closely at the finer-grained components of oral language to see if any of those components impacted the relationship between oral language and conventional literacy skills. They found that the *composite* of oral language skills had the strongest relationship with later decoding and reading comprehension. Additionally, more complex language skills like grammar and definitional vocabulary showed stronger relationships with later reading in contrast to the still relatively weak relationship of the more foundational skills of receptive and expressive vocabulary.

Because vocabulary is foundational to the learning of the more complex oral language skills, an instructional focus on vocabulary is essential. For example, a child with strong grammatical knowledge, but a limited vocabulary, would have a difficult time understanding a text or writing a meaningful narrative (as would a child with strong vocabulary and weak grammatical knowledge).

The NELP found a relatively weak relationship between vocabulary and later conventional literacy skills, particularly reading comprehension, indicating that well-developed vocabularies are necessary, but *insufficient,* for literacy. This suggests that a focus on building vocabulary alone is unlikely to be enough for improving outcomes not only in literacy, but also in oral language. It doesn't mean that vocabulary is unimportant, but that vocabulary instruction *must be accompanied by instruction in the more complex oral language skills*.

The NELP found a significant moderate effect for the category of interventions that focused on improving oral language. There was a great deal of variation in the interventions and they were implemented in a variety of ways, but usually in small groups. In addition, the interventions were delivered by different individuals, including teachers, parents, clinicians, graduate student trainees, or home visitors.

Receptive vocabulary: words needed for understanding what is heard and read

Expressive vocabulary: words used for speaking and writing

Definitional vocabulary: the bank of words for which meanings are understood

Grammar: the standard organizational rules governing language

Syntax: the rules that govern how sentences are organized and the order and relationships of words

As was true for code-focused interventions, there were no differences in the impact across the oral language studies relative to characteristics of socioeconomic status, ethnicity, or population density. As might be expected, many of the studies for this category, included populations of children who had language impairments, but results showed no significant difference in the intervention effects between children who had language impairments and those who did not. There were no differential effects based on whether the interventions were delivered by parents or teachers and whether they were play-based (where children had opportunities to choose how to become engaged with available toys) or not.

However, there was a key finding from this category related to age. There were enough studies for the panel to be able to examine any differences according to the ages of the children included in the interventions. The NELP found that oral language interventions for children in the 0-3-year-old age range were more effective than interventions for 3-5-year-old children. This finding suggests that intervening earlier rather than later is more advantageous for enhancing children's language development.

Oral Language Instruction

Some believe that language development occurs naturally and cannot be taught, but research indicates that it *can* be taught and enhanced in a variety of ways. Children start learning language from birth and, as reported by the NELP, intervening early significantly boosts young children's language development.

In an early childhood classroom, oral language learning occurs as a result of both formal and informal instructional opportunities and interactions. Children engage in conversations during independent play and through planned experiences with both adults and peers. These opportunities exist throughout all areas of the classroom and in a variety of ways. For example, in the dramatic play area children talk about and talk like the characters they portray – their feelings, actions, and ideas. Similarly, at the science center the teacher may be encouraging and modeling verbal descriptions of interesting natural objects that were collected from a trip to the park the previous day. The teacher intentionally introduces new vocabulary, tells what those words mean, and uses them in sentences to describe the objects. She also might use specific questions she has developed prior to implementing the lesson to engage children in the uses of oral language and encourage the development of their skills. Changing materials and supplies throughout the classroom and in learning centers stimulates new conversations that result in new forms of play and learning and new forms and ways of using language. Language gives words to children's thoughts, feelings, and abilities and expands their understanding of themselves, others, and the world.

All preschool children benefit from instruction focused on enhancing oral language. They can be learning many oral language skills at the same time. Direct instruction provides opportunities for children to learn new vocabulary, new concepts, definitions and synonyms for words, and to use this rich language in meaningful contexts.

Teachers play a critical role in providing diverse opportunities for children to practice and master these oral language skills, while also guiding children's oral language development with explicit and intentional instruction. They must consciously introduce new words, but also ensure that children are receiving instruction and support for developing more complex oral language skills, like definitional vocabulary, grammar, and syntax. Children who have larger vocabularies are usually better readers, but they also must have an understanding of word meanings and word usage. Their basic vocabulary needs to expand to include words that might be encountered less frequently, but that are still important to know both receptively and expressively. Children can have large receptive vocabularies which enable them to read well, but if they do not have a corresponding definitional vocabulary, their reading comprehension suffers.

Strategies that Enhance Oral Language

Strategies for supporting children's oral language development fall into two overarching categories – scaffolding and narrative talk.

Scaffolding. When adults use conversations to expand children's knowledge, they are using a technique known as scaffolding. Scaffolding means providing the support children need to reach a slightly higher level of skill – giving them opportunities to build on and extend their current skills. Teachers have chances to scaffold children's learning during instruction – modeling, questioning, and providing feedback for a child's performance.

> **Scaffolding:** providing support at a level just above children's current skill level that pushes them to a slightly higher level of skill

Modeling:
an instructional strategy of demonstrating "the behaviors, skills, and competencies that students are to learn"

In early childhood classrooms, teachers regularly schedule and plan instruction that explains and guides learning about specific content or topics. These "guided exercises, lessons, and materials that are used to teach a subject" (Collins III & O'Brien, 2003, p. 181) can include techniques such as **modeling.** Through modeling, teachers demonstrate "the behaviors, skills, and competencies that students are to learn" (Collins III & O'Brien, 2003, p. 224).

Skillful questioning can be used to engage children in learning, keep a conversation going, informally assess children's understanding, and identify the need for further instruction, modeling, or practice. Questions used by teachers can range from simple recall questions (who, what, where, when, why, and how) to open-ended questions that can result in a number of acceptable responses. Children can become personally connected to what they are learning through **distancing** questions. When teachers ask distancing questions – "In our story, Suzie seems really sad because she can't find her kitten. Has there ever been a time when you have felt really sad? What made you feel sad?" – children can relate the story to their own experiences and feelings.

Distancing:
a questioning technique that personally connects the listener to feelings and events being discussed

Providing feedback is a technique teachers can use to share information with a child about his performance. When based on observations of and interactions with the child, feedback can reinforce behavior and encourage and extend learning. Feedback also can signal a need for further explanation or modeling of a particular skill. For example, repeating a child's words emphasizes what was said and is an effective way to provide positive feedback. If a response indicates the child does not understand, the teacher can point to contextual clues that will help the child self-correct. The adult may choose to state the correct response, but needs to describe the thinking process behind it.

Narrative talk. When adults and children have a conversation, they are engaging in narrative talk. Adults can support children's oral language development through these conversations by responding to what children say, asking for additional information, and inserting new words into the discussion. Narrative talk allows adults to provide examples of words and their meanings within a context where the words have an understandable real-life application. For example, an adult can verbally describe preparing scrambled eggs, but when scrambling eggs is described while actually preparing them, children can see how to crack the egg, the egg yolk and egg white, the transformation when beating the egg before pouring it into a hot skillet, and what happens as it cooks and is turned with a spatula. The new words and the process make more sense when described within the context of the actual activity. *Spatula* can be explained and seen as a flat utensil useful for turning or flipping eggs over so that they are cooked on both sides. The word "spatula" may now be a part of not only the child's receptive and expressive vocabulary, but also of his definitional vocabulary.

> **Narrative talk:** the practice in which children and adults engage in conversations

There are many intentional opportunities to provide oral language support within everyday classroom routines and planned instruction. In general, the NELP reported that oral language instruction is best delivered in small groups or one-on-one with children.

Embedding Oral Language Activities into Daily Experiences

Teachers can help build young children's vocabulary using scaffolding and narrative talk. Here are examples of how teachers can implement these instructional strategies with children.

Before a child is talking, use narrative talk in the following ways:
- Model early words. When a child babbles early sounds (such as saying "ah"), make eye contact with the child and respond by repeating the sound and introducing a second sound (/*m*/), then combining both to say a simple two-syllable word, *ma-ma* (Hamilton, 1977).
- Use parallel talk. Describe what the child is doing in simple terms: "Hug the bunny" or "Eat the cracker" (Robertson & Weismer, 1999).
- Attach a label (name) to an object or an action. Teach the word "dog" by

saying, "Dog. Here's the dog." Use comments such as "Good dog" or "Pat the dog" or "The dog is barking." Repeating the word many times in response to the child's interest or activity develops familiarity with the word in a meaningful context (Girolametto, Pearce, & Weitzman, 1996).

- Practice self talk. "Think aloud" to describe whatever you are thinking or doing. "I'm going to change your diaper. First we take off the wet one and then put on a dry one." This is a simple strategy to support the development of vocabulary and grammar.

When a child is beginning to talk, add these activities to those described above as ways to use scaffolding and narrative talk to improve oral language skills:

- Expand language. Expand on a child's simple word. When a child says "gog" (referring to a dog), respond by saying "The dog barks" or "Furry dog." (Robertson & Weismer, 1999).
- Recast. Repeat the child's words and expand them into a complete sentence. If a child says "more dink" or "eat," add more information – "You want more juice to drink, don't you?" or "That's right. The very hungry caterpillar is eating through the apple." (Robertson & Weismer, 1999).

As a child begins to string words together, continue to use scaffolding and narrative talk by adding the following activities to those described above:

- Expand language. Expand on a child's words. When a child utters a phrase or sentence, such as "Read me book" while handing over a book, expand on the words, saying "Good idea! Let's read this interesting book all about animals and how they use their different body parts." Encourage the child to repeat the additional information by saying, "So tell me what this book is about." and the child might respond, "Animals and animal parts" (Robertson & Weismer, 1999).
- Initiate reciprocal communication. An adult can make a game of observing and catching a child's eye as he mimics the child's play using similar materials. When the child initiates another play experience, the adult names materials and describes his actions, encouraging the child to take a turn communicating within the context and safety of "the game." (Smith & Fluck, 2000). "You are placing the square blocks on top of the building to make it even taller. What block will you use next?"
- Ask open-ended questions. Ask questions that have many different

appropriate responses and encourage narrative conversation on a child's part. Open-ended questions encourage the use of more complex skills. Open-ended questions might begin with "What if…" or "What might happen…" or invite a child to "Tell me about…"

Once a child is communicating verbally and pronouncing words correctly, combine and apply all of these strategies to help boost oral language proficiency. To this add an intentional focus for teaching more complex oral language skills. Look within a variety of contexts for experiences to support oral language skills in meaningful ways.

- Use complete sentences when communicating with children and use more complex language, both directly with children and indirectly through overheard conversations with other adults. This can be done across all classroom areas throughout the day.
- The different contexts within daily routines and settings provide opportunities for conversations where adults can scaffold children's oral language learning. At snack and mealtime, teachers can initiate conversations about nutrition, ingredients, and food preparation tools and processes that apply new words and expand learning. A child's declaration that something is "good" could be expanded to "it is delicious." A teacher might encourage a child to describe what makes something "yucky" – the texture, the bitterness, or the color.
- Identify the implements used for serving, such as a "ladle" and then later sing the song "Aichen Drum" and ask if anyone remembers what a ladle is.
- In the block area, help children name and even label their airplane garage as a *hangar* and the airport as a *terminal* while helping them understand the definitions of those words.
- Field trips are another way to incorporate new words and uses of words. A visit to the zoo incorporates an entire vocabulary specific to that environment, with names of animals (e.g., specific types of primates, such as baboons and gorillas), animal characteristics (e.g., nocturnal, cold-blooded), and their habitats (e.g., desert, polar). Look within the contexts of all experiences for meaningful ways to boost oral language skills.

Teachers must have an understanding of the sequence and developmental expectations for oral language learning if they are going to assess and monitor oral language development. They are then able to listen to and observe various indicators that children are making appropriate progress and adjust instruction to model and provide support as needed.

Teachers:

- Observe and listen for children to increase the quantity and duration of conversations with adults and each other.
- Listen for children's use of new words and their understanding of word meanings.
- Note children's ability to retell stories.
- Observe children's language during free choice activities, such as their interactions with other children in the dramatic play area.

Summary

Research indicates that intentionally and explicitly applying proven strategies for supporting oral language at each stage of a young child's development has moderate to significant impact on oral language acquisition, which is important for developing later skills in conventional literacy areas of reading, writing, and spelling.

Below are some key points regarding oral language learning.

- Oral language programs and instructional approaches are important for early childhood classrooms because oral language allows children to communicate with others. Oral language development influences the successful growth of the conventional literacy skills of reading, writing, and spelling.
- Definitional vocabulary, listening comprehension, and grammar have a strong relationship with later reading and writing.
- Most early oral language experiences occur during conversations between adults and children within the meaningful context of daily routines and activities relevant to children's lives. Oral language development can be measurably advanced through explicit, intentional instruction.
- Supporting children's oral language development should begin at birth, and the level of complexity should be scaffolded as children become more skilled.
- As with other literacy categories, oral language instruction was shown to be

effective when taught one-on-one or in a small group. There was no evidence that it was effective when taught in large group settings.

- Children are more likely to succeed at learning to speak when they are given opportunities to hear many words being used in a variety of ways and when they are encouraged to develop their own oral language skills through many opportunities to practice using words to express their own ideas.

- Although there is no evidence that vocabulary instruction by itself results in better conventional literacy outcomes, it is the foundation for more complex oral language skills and is a critically important aspect of development that allows children to communicate with others. Instruction needs to focus on more than just vocabulary.

- Oral language instruction should include regularly scheduled practice that incorporates modeling and both guided and independent practice.

What Is Shared Reading?

Shared reading is a reading strategy where the adult actively involves a child or small group of children in reading a book. Strategies used during this reading introduce conventions of print and new vocabulary words, and encourage predictions, rhyming, discussion of pictures, and other interactive experiences. Although shared reading is often recommended as the single most important thing adults can do to promote the emergent literacy skills of young children, a summary of studies that examined the effect of shared reading on young children's emergent literacy skills called into question these positive effects. (Scarborough & Dobrich, 1994). Accordingly, the National Early Literacy Panel (NELP) examined the effects of interventions that focused on shared reading. The various approaches to shared reading in the studies reviewed by the NELP differed in their interactive focus. Shared reading can be as simple as an adult reading a book to a child, but can also be an opportunity for teachers to introduce new words in the context of the book

> **Shared reading:** a reading strategy where the adult involves a child or small group of children in reading a book that introduces conventions of print and new vocabulary, or encourages predictions, rhyming, discussion of pictures, and other interactive experiences

content or story, explain the definition, and embed those same words in extended conversation about the book and in later conversations.

What Are the Key Findings Regarding Shared Reading?

The NELP found that "sharing books with young children has a *significant, substantial, and positive impact* both on young children's oral language skills and on young children's print knowledge" (NELP, 2008, p. 155). Although a limited number of studies prevented the analysis of the impact of socioeconomic status, ethnicity, or population density, the NELP concluded that shared reading is appropriate and effective for a very diverse group of young children. It worked equally well with children who were at risk of later reading difficulties and those who were not, as well as with younger and older children. Additionally, both parents and teachers can effectively implement shared reading when taught proven strategies.

Interventions that used a more interactive style of shared reading had a stronger impact on children's oral language skills than did non-interactive approaches. In particular, dialogic reading, an approach where the adult facilitates the child's active role in telling the story, proved to be highly effective.

No studies provided evidence that shared reading by itself is sufficient for promoting children's later conventional literacy skills, including their ability to read. Therefore, it is recommended that shared reading should be paired with other early literacy instructional practices to provide the greatest impact for preparing children to be successful readers.

Interactive Shared Reading

The overall evidence for shared reading supports approaches that are more intensive in frequency and interactive in their style. Interactive shared reading is a perfect example of the power of an integrated focus for learning – it's a great way to intentionally include strategies for enhancing children's oral language and print awareness. For example, teachers can use shared reading to introduce new concepts, boost vocabulary growth, and point out characteristics of print.

The shared reading process as described in effective studies included in the NELP Report were implemented one-on-one or in small groups. However, early childhood classroom teachers often read books aloud during circle time with the whole class. Until there is evidence of whether or not this is effective, it is recommended that teachers plan for and provide one-on-one and small group interactive shared reading opportunities in the early childhood classroom and incorporate similar strategies when reading to larger groups. While each child is less involved with the story in large group shared reading, teachers should continue to apply strategies that engage and hold children's interest, such as giving voices to the characters and reading with expression. Below is a description of types of things to do in an interactive shared reading experience.

Before reading:

- Carefully select a book that has: rich narrative, interesting or novel content, rich detailed illustrations, appropriate and challenging vocabulary that includes new or unusual words, and the potential for different points of view.
- Read through the selection and identify places where you will introduce targeted vocabulary words. Plan how to define the words and identify objects or pictures that represent the words. Be sure to include unusual or infrequently used words.
- Before beginning to read, show objects and pictures as ways to introduce new words. Ask questions, such as "What is this?" and then "What can I do with this?" or "Tell me what you know about this?" Later, props that support the vocabulary words can be added to learning centers. For example, if reading *The Carrot Seed* by Ruth Krauss, the teacher might have available items such as seeds, a shovel, a rake, a watering can, and a carrot. An unusual word to teach could be *sprinkle*.

During reading:

- The first time you read a new book to children, read it without using any specific strategies. Read the book to children so that they can get familiar with the content and story.
- When reading the second time around, read expressively.
- Focus vocabulary words, encouraging the children to identify the word and explain the word meaning within the context of the story.

- Ask questions to promote discussion about content to support listening comprehension. The types of questions asked will depend on children's developmental skills. For example, some questions (such as "What is that?") elicit a brief response compared to questions that encourage a more narrative response (such as "Why do you think…?").
- Encourage participation by praising and supporting the child's response, "That's right. The puppy looks sad." and encourage more guided oral language practice with extension questions, such as "Why do you think he looks sad?"
- Follow this process at identified points during the shared reading (Valdez-Menchaca & Whitehurst, 1992; Morrow, O'Connor, & Smith, 1990).

After reading:

- Check listening comprehension with targeted questions and by having children retell elements of the story, remembering the sequence of events and important details. Allow children to use story props to re-enact the story.
- This is a great time for children to express opinions and make connections between events in the story and similar experiences they have had.
- To extend the concepts and themes in the book, provide related materials and activities. For example, with *The Carrot Seed,* children might look at a variety of seeds; make a book picturing seeds we eat, such as beans, corn, poppy seeds, nuts, and peas; or do a planting or cooking activity (Wasik & Bond, 2001).

Further ideas for actively engaging preschoolers in interactive shared book reading include repeating exposures to the same book; discussing new words and features of the book, such as the title, cover, and pictures before book reading; and citing experiences that extend the concepts and themes in the book after reading. For example, books related to food can suggest grocery shopping trips, cooking experiences, or a meal at a restaurant, while books about animals might result in singing songs and saying animal rhymes or taking a walk in the neighborhood, a city park, or the zoo to observe a variety of animals.

Dialogic Reading

One particularly effective form of interactive shared reading that showed significant results is dialogic reading (Whitehurst, et al., 1988). Both teachers and parents can be trained with videotapes and practice reading experiences in short sessions to implement this strategy. The label "dialogic reading" implies a dialog or conversation while reading.

This specific type of shared book reading is also addressed in a separate What Works Clearinghouse intervention report (U.S. Department of Education, What Works Intervention Report, Shared Reading, updated April 2015). During dialogic reading, the adult uses a specific approach to prompt children while reading a book. The adult becomes both active listener and questioner, enabling adult and child to switch roles so that the child learns to become the storyteller.

This strategy is based on three broad principles: (a) encourage the child to participate, (b) provide feedback to the child, and (c) adapt the reading style to the child's growing linguistic abilities. An acronym to help adults remember the dialogic reading process is called **PEER**. **P**rompt the child with a question about the story, such as "What is that animal?" **E**valuate and **E**xpand on the child's response. If the child says, "It's a dog" you might say "Yes, it's a dog called a dachshund." **R**epeat the initial question to check that the child understands the new information. "So tell me what that animal is?" Finally, build upon the child's interests and linguistic abilities by encouraging talk about other features of the book unfamiliar to the child, such as words, characters, and concepts.

There are five basic types of prompts adults use to encourage dialog about a book. The word **CROWD** stands for the types of questions used in dialogic reading. This is not a quiz, but a way to engage the child in a conversation about the book.
- *Completion questions* encourage the child to finish a phrase or sentence in the story – "Brown bear, brown bear, _____?"
- *Recall questions* help check the child's understanding of story content – "What did the brown bear see first?"
- *Open-ended questions* increase the amount of dialog about a book and focus on details encouraging a narrative response rather than a mere "yes" or "no" or nonverbal pointing. For example, you might ask a child to describe what is happening on a particular page.

- *"Wh" questions* (who, what, where, when, and why) can help teach new vocabulary and stimulate a child's use of language and novel speech.
- D*istancing questions* encourage children to connect the pictures and words in the book to experiences outside the story – "How is the puppy in this story like our dog, Spot?"

Books that are already familiar work well, since the dialogic reading strategy is not recommended for the first reading of a story. Storybooks with a rich narrative and plenty of action work best, keeping in mind that the quantity of text needs to be less for a younger child. Books that include new words provide an opportunity to build vocabulary and the content supports learning about new information. Children are far more engaged if they find the book interesting, and that is determined by topic as well as the use of rich detailed illustrations.

Providing a Focus on Vocabulary Through Shared Reading

A more intensive and intentional focus on vocabulary instruction can be included as part of shared reading routines in the early childhood classroom. The process for learning a new word typically includes several stages. The first stage for learning a word is when the word is totally new – "I never saw it before." The next time a word is heard, the child might think, "I've heard it, but I don't know what it means." In the third stage, the child might recognize the word and know that it relates to information within a particular context. The final stage is when a word is solidly represented in the child's vocabulary; when she has the feeling that "I know it!" Reaching this point is influenced by how many times a word is encountered, the type of word, and if the word is supported by visual or concrete associations. Some words are easier to learn and remember than others. Words that can be connected to something concrete are easier to understand and know than abstract words, so supporting the introduction of new words with visuals and concrete objects is important. This process for intentionally learning vocabulary can be incorporated into early childhood classrooms.

Definitional vocabulary – understanding the meanings of words – is an essential part of the process for increasing children's vocabulary. Specifically, teachers can explain, use simpler words, or provide a different context in order to help children understand the meaning of new words. Lower frequency words that are important for children to learn can be incorporated into instruction through conversations and interactive book reading where adults are modeling the use of words in more complex sentence structures. Within the shared reading experience, identify a word that is the focus for learning (note that there may be several words to focus upon). For instance, in Mo Willems book *Knuffle Bunny*, teachers might focus on the word *laundromat*. Talk about what the word means within the context of the story. In this example, picture clues can help a child learn the meaning of *laundromat* if the child has no related prior experience. Encourage the child to understand this word within the broader context of prior knowledge or personal experiences. If the child has never been to a *laundromat*, the idea of doing laundry still may be familiar and spur discussion. Revisit the word within the shared reading experience, as it fits with the story, and also in discussion after the story. The word can be included while doing the family wash and a trip to a *laundromat* would be another way to establish clearer understanding.

New words that are learned in shared reading experiences can be extended into other activities occurring in the early childhood classroom. Repeated readings allow words to be heard and practiced. Then intentionally incorporate that word into conversations and other situations within the early childhood setting in order to provide the frequent use necessary for a child to "own" the new word.

Making Books Available in the Early Childhood Classroom

To effectively promote children's experiences with books in the early childhood classroom, a number and variety of books must be available for them to use. As a way for children to independently explore books and book-related materials, many classrooms have a library area. This area can include items such as books, magazines, videos, audio-recorded stories, big books, view masters, felt board characters, and puppets. It also can include materials for creating books, such as paper, markers, glue, crayons, and pencils.

Because reading is generally a quiet activity, locate the library area where there is little traffic or noise. Make it comfortable with cushions, a sofa or soft chairs, or a rocker. Good lighting is important and an extra lamp might also provide a home-like atmosphere. If possible, display books with the covers facing out, so children can see the selections without having to pull them off the shelf. Have an assortment of 25 – 30 picture books that represent a variety of types or genres (stories, non-fiction, poetry, fairy tales, concept, alphabet, etc.) and levels, from wordless books or books with very few words, to books with several sentences or a paragraph per page. Change the books in this area every few weeks so that children have time to revisit a favorite story as well as anticipate new books to explore. Local libraries typically allow teachers to check out large numbers of books and often are willing to pull together a collection of specific titles or books related to a particular topic or theme. Notice books that seem to be children's favorites and use that information to help with future selections. Bring in more books by the same authors, books that are similar in style or type, or that provide information about a topic of particular interest to you and the children.

Many classrooms have a lending library where parents and children can take books home for shared reading experiences. These can be library books, books that belong to your classroom, or purchased kits that include books with read-aloud suggestions and some kits that include materials to expand learning related to the book, such as a puppet, stuffed toy, or other related prop.

It is also beneficial for books to be integrated in all of the other areas of the classroom. The block area might have books with rich illustrations of buildings specific to your topic of learning. If you are studying transportation, you might include books with pictures of bridges, airports, garages, superhighways and railroads. Maybe you will want to include an instruction manual for building with Lego blocks. In the science area, you might have a book about animals or colors. If the dramatic play area has been turned into a beauty shop, you might include magazines with hairstyles. And for art, you might want books about famous artists that show their masterpieces, or books with illustrated directions for building a clay sculpture. These materials should all be introduced in order for children to know they are available.

As a way to reinforce book experiences, take five to ten minutes at the end of the day to discuss and summarize that day's story reading activities (Morrow, O'Connor, & Smith, 1990).

Summary

Just reading aloud to children does not necessarily mean they will become successful readers. How a read-aloud is conducted is very important in developing young children's early language and literacy skills. Most importantly, reading aloud to children must be accompanied by other forms of intentional and effective instructional strategies.

Shared reading is a successful approach for advancing the development of young children's oral language skills and print knowledge. It can be implemented with an individual child or with a small group of children. Both parents and teachers can provide shared reading experiences.

Interactive shared reading, an approach that attempts to engage the child in the reading experience, is more effective than a non-interactive approach. The adult plans in advance the best ways to engage the child, such as choosing specific words and skills to focus upon, pointing to elements of print, and including opportunities to check for listening comprehension.

An example of a highly effective interactive approach is called dialogic reading. To implement dialogic reading, adults encourage the child to participate in a conversation about a book by asking questions, thinking about the child's response, and providing feedback that promotes and adapts to the child's learning.

The limited number of studies in the shared reading category did not reveal if there are any other benefits to shared reading. The analysis of so few studies showed no evidence that shared reading promotes other early literacy skills or improves later conventional literacy skills. It is also important to note that learning about the impact of other factors on shared reading results, such as children's age, socioeconomic status, and ethnicity; who implemented the shared reading strategies; if they are effective with large groups; and how long the programs lasted, will require more studies that monitor these characteristics. Based on current information, therefore, shared reading strategies are effective for a broad range of children.

What Are the Key Findings Regarding Parents' Role in Supporting Children's Early Language and Literacy Development?

The NELP Report included an evaluation of parent and home programs that focused on learning the extent to which strategies used by parents could be attributed to improving children's early language and literacy development. Parent and home programs had moderate to large effects on children's oral language and cognitive abilities. However, there was large variation in the focus of the interventions, making it difficult to identify approaches that might be most effective.

Although there were a number of studies included in this category, few studies had a similar focus, making it difficult for panelists to analyze key aspects of the programs, examine parent influences for each category, and generalize as to the programs' effects on children's skills. More research is needed to identify aspects of programs and pinpoint parent practices that are effective for impacting children's skill development.

Following reported indications that there is a link between parental involvement and children's early literacy-related development, the panel conducted its study of these interventions with the understanding that "successful parental involvement programs help parents understand the importance of their role as first teachers and equip them with both the skills and the strategies to foster their children's language and literacy development" (NELP, 2008, p. 173). Given the limited number of studies, there were no indications of significant differences in effectiveness based on whether or not materials were provided or based on children's ages and the demographic characteristics of their families, such as socioeconomic status, ethnicity, or population density. What programs did have in common, however, is that parents were responsible for implementing the strategies and they had been instructed and supervised on the implementation of the strategies by the developers themselves.

What Can Parents Do to Support Children's Early Language and Literacy Development?

While this is not intended to imply that parents should not be doing other things, there are things that parents do that have shown measureable effects on children's early language and literacy development. These things are primarily in the areas of oral language and shared reading.

Parents have many opportunities to support their child's language development, particularly within the 0-3 ages where strategies are shown to have the greatest effect. Within the meaningful context of natural settings, parents can initiate interactions and respond to their child in ways that boost vocabulary and complex oral language skills. This can be done where parents expand on their child's language and knowledge within conversations. Parents can use regular routines within the home setting for: modeling appropriate language skills, labeling objects and actions, and describing what they or their child is doing; recasting the child's words in ways that expand language and apply more complex skills; and by asking questions that encourage thinking and talking. When parents provide a variety of experiences, their child is exposed to words and their uses that are specific to the experience or setting. For example, the types of language and activities experienced when at church, the zoo, shopping, at a park, and visiting friends and relatives may differ from the language and activities that take place at home.

Interactive shared reading is another highly effective way for parents to build a child's vocabulary and cognitive abilities. Books often include new words and structures that are different from language typically used in conversations. Following the dialogic reading process, parents can prompt their child with questions, evaluate and expand on the response, provide feedback, and adapt to the child's interests and abilities. Repeated exposures to the same book allow parents to discuss concepts at new and deeper levels, note print features of the book and revisit words for building vocabulary as well as other complex oral language skills. When a book is reread, the conversation about it can be expanded with more complex types of questions and a child can become more confident and competent in the comfortable setting of its familiarity. Providing a variety of books is a way for parents to diversify their child's experiences with language, structure, and information.

How Can Teachers Help Parents Support Their Children's Early Language and Literacy Development?

Teachers can help parents learn effective ways to support their children's early learning by sharing information, making materials available, and modeling strategies. They can have age-appropriate books available for parents with information about how children can benefit from, enjoy, and interact with books, and they can provide a demonstration or information on how to read aloud with a young child (High, LaGasse, Becker, Ahlgren, & Gardner, 2000). A lending library that is available to parents can include information about why it's important to read aloud with a young child, with suggestions for ways to engage a child in the read-aloud process.

Parents can be taught types of questions to ask and the process to follow for implementing the dialogic reading strategy (Arnold, Lonigan, Whitehurst, & Epstein, 1994).

Newsletters, tip sheets, and Web sites are ways information and strategies can be shared with parents. These tools can be strengthened by demonstrations and workshops where parents are allowed to see and practice recommended strategies. When parents are taught specific reading strategies, and they use those strategies with their children in tandem with teachers—children benefit. (Senechal, 2006).

Summary

Parent and home programs were found to have significant effects on children's oral language and cognitive abilities. Although there were a number of studies that examined parent and home programs, it was difficult to pinpoint specific programs and practices that were effective because the studies varied widely so that no program or practice stood out.

What is important is the impact parents can have on their children. Teachers can help parents support their children's language and literacy development by providing information and experiences that facilitate the quality and quantity of that support. Children benefit when parents learn simple and effective strategies for supporting their development. Teachers can help parents learn these strategies by sharing information, demonstrating simple activities, and providing opportunities for guided practice.

Information can be shared in newsletters, on Web sites, and at parent-teacher conferences. Teachers can provide brief demonstrations at a school open-house or as a regular part of meetings and other school events. Workshops and short training events can include information, modeling, and guided practice.

Children's first language experiences typically occur at home with their families. When parents apply strategies, such as self talk, parallel talk, expanding and recasting children's language, they can significantly impact the quantity of words children hear and eventually use. Interactive shared reading is another way parents share language and information with children while also building book knowledge, print awareness, and cognition. In the context of meaningful family experiences within regular routines and common outings, these strategies can boost children's vocabularies and other more complex oral language skills, build print awareness and book knowledge, and promote cognitive development.

A developmentally appropriate early childhood classroom supports growth in all **developmental domains** through both play-based experiences and teacher-directed instruction. This instruction is delivered individually and in small and large groups within the context of classroom learning areas and across children's individual skill levels. There are many things to consider in order to provide high quality appropriate learning experiences and doing this well is complicated.

Developmental domains: physical, social, emotional, cognitive, and language domains that are essential to children's growth and development

What does literacy-focused instruction look like in the early childhood classroom? Teachers support play-based experiences through inviting environments and stimulating materials. They also provide **direct instruction** as an intentional planned way to support learning and development that is based on research-proven best practices.

Direct instruction: teacher-led lesson implementation that is a planned way to introduce, guide, and support children's learning of information and skills

Language and literacy instruction for children should focus on a combination of skills that are needed for becoming successful readers and writers. This instruction can be delivered in interactive ways with many opportunities for modeling and guided and independent practice. There should be regular opportunities for instruction in phonological awareness, vocabulary, concept development, print knowledge, and shared reading. The research reported by the NELP provides strong evidence that supporting the development of these foundational skills leads to the successful acquisition of reading, writing, and spelling.

The following interactive shared reading experience is a sample lesson developed from the teacher's perspective that shows ways to integrate many of these interrelated early literacy skills into one instructional event. Some of the skills supported in this lesson have been featured to show how they can be contextualized within the early childhood classroom.

A Teacher's Plan: Integrated Literacy Instruction Within Shared Reading

Trees are budding, the grass is starting to turn green, and I am planning to take my preschool class on a walk to look for signs of spring. *In the Tall, Tall Grass* by Denise Fleming was selected as a perfect fit to read with the children now, and repeat again at various points during the spring and summer. This will allow the children to revisit the story, have repeated contact with vocabulary, and make connections to their own observations and experiences in the outdoors. This book has large, vivid illustrations, minimal text in a large font, includes some words that might be new, and uses several literary devices, such as alliteration and rhyme that make it fun and a good choice for my lesson.

I read the story to myself to think about how I will use this book for literacy instruction. As many times as I've read this book, I now notice another feature – you really can't tell if the child is male or female, which is rather nice because the important thing is that it's a child who is curious and observant, and that could be any child in my classroom.

Before reading, I begin planning and start by taking a quick inventory.
- Content focuses on animals (caterpillars, hummingbirds, bees, birds, ants, snakes, moles, beetles, toads, bunnies, fireflies, bats) within a day to night timeframe. To help children make connections, I will ask them to talk about animals they commonly see outdoors and look and listen for animals when

we take our walk.

- Vocabulary includes a review of the animals as well as several unusual words to introduce – *munch, dart, strum, lug, glide, skitter, scurry, lunge, swoop*. That's really too many to discuss in one reading, so I'll have to identify just a few to focus on.

- Rhyme elements, such as *crunch/munch/lunch*; *strum/drum/hum*; *snap/flap*; *tug/lug*; *go* and *glow*; *bright* and *moonlight* exist on most pages. After the children have heard the story once or twice they should be able to join in saying some of these rhyming words, supporting phonological awareness and memory.

- Alliteration is also used throughout the book, creating the possibility for blending practice and supporting alphabet knowledge. Examples include: *dart/dip*; *slip/slide/snakes*; *skitter/scurry*; *zip/zap*; *hip/hop*; *lunge/loop*. I won't want to point out all of these in one reading, but will select a few and save some for another time.

- This book also has examples of sound words (onomatopoeia) such as *crunch, hum, snap, ritch, ratch, zap*.

- The large type provides a good opportunity to focus on letters of the alphabet, and I will select a few beginning letters to identify, probably within the examples of alliteration. *Z* might be a good one since you so seldom see it used, and *s* is repeated in many places. I might emphasize these similar sounds but will make sure to pronounce them clearly so children can hear the difference.

- The large type and the way it slants and curves to match the words is great for supporting print awareness. I can point to these words as I read. Also, the print appears at different places within the pictures, yet it is bold and distinctly different from the pictures themselves.

- Finally, I think about any visuals or props I might want to use in teaching the lesson. An insect finger puppet might be nice to use; several instruments that make some of the corresponding sounds may enhance an explanation of the words, and I know I will need chart paper for phonological awareness instruction and introducing vocabulary, plus a blank index card for covering up parts of words. I add small sticky notes to remind myself of specific vocabulary words to teach or literary devices I don't want to forget to point out.

During reading

Before showing the book, I lead children in an analysis activity using the words *strum*, *drum* and *hum*. These words are printed on chart paper in a column. I then ask the children to be detectives and look for letters that appear in all three words. "That's right. They all have the same ending, -um." I cover the onset of each word with the index card and we read the rime, "-um, -um, -um." Showing the whole words and pointing, I clearly pronounce each word and each time ask the children to repeat; then we read through the list of words once more. I explain that all three words have to do with sounds and we talk about how the sounds are made. *Strum* is a new word and I strum my fingers on a table several times. Children demonstrate drumming their hands on the carpet. I hum and then we all hum together. I ask children to show how to softly make these sounds and we practice each one more time.

Phonological awareness

Focus on content

I then ask my small group of children to tell me about recent changes they have noticed outdoors. This is an open-ended discussion and the small group of children means that each child has an opportunity to contribute. I listen, evaluate their responses and expand on their words by adding a few descriptors. "I've noticed that the trees are budding, too. Has anyone heard or seen any animals this spring? Where might you look?" I explain that the book we're going to read is about animals they may see this spring and summer. "Many animals have a particular way to move and they also might make different sounds. What animals might hum like we just did?" "One animal we're going to see in this book moves in an unusual way. I then introduce the new or unusual words used to describe the bats' movements. I write each word on the chart paper and gesture with my hands to demonstrate while saying the words – lunge (dive), loop (circle) and swoop (fly down). "What kind of animal might lunge, loop and swoop?" I praise children for contributing ideas and suggest we search as we read our book.

Introducing new or unusual vocabulary

Now I show the book and ask if anyone remembers reading it before. Pointing to the title, I slowly read (encouraging those who remember to read along with me), *In the Tall, Tall Grass*, and then point to the author's name and say "by Denise Fleming. This is the person who wrote and also

Listening comprehension and making information relevant to children's lives

Print awareness

illustrated this book. What does *illustrated* mean?" I then show the front and back and ask children to tell me what they think this book is about. On the title page I again point to the words and together we read "*In the Tall, Tall Grass* by Denise Fleming." We read the first page together because these are the same words as the title and should now be a bit familiar – they may recognize some of the letters and the shapes of the words and once I start they are able to help complete the phrase. As I turn the page I say, "Ooh. What does he see first? That's right – brightly colored caterpillars!" and read, pointing to the words, some slanting to emphasize where the caterpillars have eaten. I read the next page, again pointing to the letters and then ask if anyone has seen a hummingbird. Since no one has, I explain that they are tiny birds and ask children to hold out their hands, explaining that these birds are smaller than their hand. I encourage them to look carefully at the picture to note characteristics of the bird – the long beak used to sip (like a straw that the children use to sip) and the wings that flap so fast that it looks like they have more than two. They also note the bright colors and the ruby-colored throat.

As we read the pages about the bees, I point to the words and several children recognize the words we looked at earlier and read them with me – "strum, drum, bees hum."

I continue reading expressively, emphasizing the sounds the words make, and as we get to the pages with toads and then the bunnies, I point to the sky and ask the children if they notice anything happening – it's no longer bright and sunny, and maybe it now has turned to evening. When we get to the pages with the bats, I read slowly, "lunge, loop" and encourage the children to use the picture to help finish reading "bats swoop," identifying the **Vocabulary** animal that makes the movements we spoke about earlier. Children try out the animal actions and "swoop," "lunge," and "loop" using body movements to help define these new words.

After reading

When we finish the story I pause as one child says, "I like that story" and another agrees. I ask them to describe the part they liked best and afterwards we decide to think about all the animals mentioned. We list them on **Listening comprehension, narrative, language, vocabulary** chart paper and I ask children to remember the sound and movements the animals make, **Alphabet knowledge** encouraging the use of the exact words used in the book. When writing down *zip* and *zap*, I say the words, point and ask children to name the beginning letter. This is done with several other words as well. I then mention that we are going to go for a walk later that day and suggest we look for animals and listen for sounds. They might do the same thing at home that evening and tomorrow we will add new words to our list.

While on our walk, I comment on some of the sounds I notice, finding some of the same sounds and actions made by other things. I see a bird *swoop* to pick up a scrap of bread and point out the *whir* of a passing car. I think back on the lesson and reflect on where I might be ready to scaffold some skills that are mastered and where other skills may need additional instruction. I think about each child's participation and note that several had difficulty with the synthesis activity and alphabet knowledge. Those will be areas of focus in next lessons, but we will continue to practice mastered skills as we add new ones. We'll do another synthesis activity with *sip/dip* – simple words that differ only in onset. I've posted our chart paper and we will revisit words for word meaning and phonological awareness as we add new words to the list. The next reading of this book will include a focus on other words and I will liven things up with several puppets – the children can use these to demonstrate the animal movements named in the book, and the puppets will then go into the dramatic play area to extend the experience. This author has written a similar book and that might be an opportunity to think about the author/illustrator's style. In fact, a series of lessons around her books might be a great springboard for new learning.

Print awareness, book knowledge

A Teacher's Plan: Code-focused Literacy Instruction

The following is an example of a small group code-focused lesson from the teacher's perspective. This lesson focuses on the synthesis skill of blending. A similar process can be followed for other code-focused lessons.

Before the Lesson

Based on formal and informal assessment, I decided that the lesson for this particular small group of children will focus on blending phonemes to make words. This is an important skill for being able to read. We will practice with one-syllable words that have no more than two or three letters. I checked several online lists of high-frequency words for new readers, figuring these words will be a good place to start and identified the following words for our beginning lesson: *in*, *an*, *at* and *it*. I make letter cards for creating the following words using these four words as the rime, such as *pin, tin, fin, kin, bin, din; ban, can, fan, pan, ran, tan; bat, fat, rat, cat, sat, hat, mat;* and *bit, fit, hit, kit, lit, nit, pit, sit, wit.*

If I use vocabulary words from *In the Tall, Tall Grass*, I can continue to expose the children to those words and strengthen their learning by combining phonological awareness with the definitions of those words through our interactive shared reading. However, many of the vocabulary words from our book, *In the Tall, Tall Grass*, begin with blends and are not suitable for this lesson. I did find some words — *tug, lug* — to use for additional practice. I added some words of my own and created the following list *tug, lug, bug, dug, hug, jug, mug, rug; hip, dip, lip, nip, pip, rip, sip, tip, zip; hop, bop, mop, pop, top; zap, cap, gap, lap, map, nap, pap, rap, sap, tap.*

We won't use all of these different onset cards in this lesson, but I will have them available for a future lesson and for children to use for independent practice. I make a set of letter cards for each child and put them in envelopes with directions for how to practice using them. These can be used for independent practice and sent home for children to use with their parents.

During the Lesson

1. First, I *define* the concept being taught. "We have been learning letter-sounds and today we're going to practice blending these together to make words."

2. Then I *model and explain.* "I'm going to show you how to blend two letter-sounds to make a word. The first step is to identify the short sound this letter makes (show the letter *i*). It's the letter *i* and it makes the /*i*/ sound like the sound in the words *igloo, iguana* and *icky*. Say that sound with me: /*i*/. Next I will identify the letter-sound the letter *n* makes. /*n*/ Let's say that letter-sound together: /*n*/. as in *n-ow* and *n-ext. N-ow*, I'm going to put the two sounds together." I hold the cards apart and move them closer together each time I say them until they are side-by-side and I say the word *in.*

3. Next I provide *guided practice*, following this same process with the words *an, at* and *it*. "Let's identify the short sound this letter makes (show the letter *a*). Right. It makes the /*a*/ sound like the sound in the words *apple, ant* and *alligator*. Say that sound with me: /*a*/. Now, what sound does this

letter make (showing the card for the letter *n*)? /*n*/ Let's say that letter-sound together. /*n*/ Let's put the two sounds together." I hold the cards apart and move them closer together each time while we say the letters until they are side-by-side and we say the word *an*.

4. During the practice, I give *feedback*. We repeat this process for the words *at,* and *it*. Each time I encourage the children to take the lead in sounding out the letters and in saying the letters together. I observe each child and notice who is actively participating and who seems to be struggling. For children who are struggling, I note if the problem is that they don't know the letter-sounds or if they are struggling with blending the letters together.

5. We end the lesson with opportunities for *independent practice*, especially using words from our story. I have some letter cards that I keep in the area where we hold small group time. Later in the day I may work individually with children who seemed to need extra practice and we review these same words.

After the Lesson

At the end of the day, each child can take home an envelope with letter cards to practice the blending activity with parents. It's important that I reflect to informally assess each child's understanding. Although we will continue practicing the skills introduced, some children may already be ready to add a consonant onset to these simple words to make other words. I think about other rimes that we might practice with (some that are words and some that are not), such as *on, ish, og, ick, ack*.

Doing what works in the provision of early language and literacy instruction is a sound decision for ensuring that young children become successful readers. The National Early Literacy Panel has identified the early literacy skills and types of instruction that can make that difference. This *What Works* guide is an introduction for teachers in translating the research findings into daily classroom practices and strategies to support families at-home, to advance children's emergent literacy development and later reading skills.

The NELP identified:
- The early literacy skills that predict later achievement in reading, writing, and spelling
- The instructional programs, practices, and approaches that impact early literacy and conventional literacy skills
- Characteristics of young learners that influence the effectiveness of the instructional programs and approaches
- Types of environments and settings that moderate the effects of the instructional programs and approaches
- Other variations in the instructional programs and approaches that influence their effectiveness

The key for early childhood teachers in providing the best language and literacy instruction for young children is to combine the results of what the NELP learned about the strongest early literacy skills that are precursors to later conventional literacy skills and from interventions that demonstrate effective instruction.

The early literacy skills that showed strong to moderate relationships with later reading, writing, and spelling and for which there is effective instructional evidence are:

- alphabet knowledge
- phonological awareness
- oral language.

Code-focused instructional approaches that teach phonological awareness, phonological awareness with alphabet knowledge, and phonological awareness with phonics are all effective in improving a broad range of children's early literacy skills and conventional literacy skills. Programs that sought to improve children's oral language were effective at doing just that. Finally, shared reading programs, especially those that applied interactive techniques, impacted children's oral language and print awareness skills. The majority of the programs and practices that worked were teacher-directed, implemented in small groups or one-on-one with children, and occurred frequently. Generally, the programs and practices were effective across a broad range of children, including children considered at risk.

Given this information, teachers can select curriculum that provides an appropriate focus for improving children's literacy development, administer assessments and monitor children's ongoing learning with a focus on the relevant skills, and plan and organize instruction in ways that will have the greatest impact for young children. Teachers also can partner with parents to encourage and support appropriate and effective literacy interactions with their children. Parents can be successful at improving their children's oral language skills through shared reading experiences and by implementing a variety of language strategies with them.

The intensity and explicitness with which teachers provide effective instruction and practices will influence how well children succeed in acquiring the skills that are essential to becoming good readers. Teachers cannot rely on a singular focus to make these improvements, but must implement an integrated instructional program that combines many effective approaches for developing a broad range of early literacy skills.

Instruction can be applied in interesting and playful ways with children and through more direct and intensive techniques in a variety of daily activities and routines across the early childhood classroom.

The National Early Literacy Panel Report clearly identifies the proven practices and programs that effectively improve children's emergent literacy and later reading achievement. Early childhood teachers and parents play a critical role in accomplishing these goals. Therefore, it is imperative that teachers are prepared and competent to deliver effective instruction and parents have the support they need to improve their children's language and literacy development. This guide offers the first steps for what works, so teachers and parents can become strong literacy leaders in defining a pathway of reading success for all young children.

The **National Center for Family Literacy** (NCFL) is the worldwide leader in family literacy, an intergenerational approach to help families escape poverty through education. More than one million families have made positive educational and economic gains as a result of NCFL's work, which includes training thousands of teachers and volunteers.

Established in 1989 by its current President, Sharon Darling, NCFL envisions a world in which all families are provided opportunities to improve their lives and become strong contributors to society. We address our nation's literacy challenges by engaging all family members in learning, beginning with the parent. NCFL is a national leader in education, with three decades of developing, implementing, and documenting innovative intergenerational strategies with research-based outcomes that have impacted millions of families. Our primary focus is to empower parents and children struggling with low literacy and language skills to become strong contributors to society. We develop, implement, and document innovative two-generation practices, networks, and learning tools. We lead and work with learners, administrators, teachers, librarians, policymakers, philanthropists, and advocates nationwide.

NCFL offers professional development on a variety of topics including:

• Early Language & Literacy Development (Birth to Five Years)
• English as a Second Language
• Family Literacy & Family Learning
• Adult Reading Instruction
• Common Core State Standards
• Community Literacy
• Parent and Family Engagement

To learn more about NCFL professional development opportunities, visit our website at www.familieslearning.org.

Alphabet knowledge: a state of familiarity with the alphabet, which is the complete set of letters or other graphic symbols representing speech sounds used in writing a language or in phonetic transcription

Alphabetic principle: the understanding that letters are used to represent speech sounds (phonemes) and that there is a systematic and predictable relationship between written letters and spoken words

Analysis: breaking or taking apart

Causation: something that produces an effect; figuring out why something happened

Code-focused skills: the abilities of phonological awareness, alphabet knowledge, and early decoding or phonics

Cognitive operation: the learning task children are performing on sound units

Computer-assisted instruction: computer-based learning programs that present content sequentially, request responses from the learner and provide immediate feedback for each response

Concepts about print: knowledge of print conventions (e.g., left-right, front-back) and concepts (book cover, author, text)

Conventional literacy skills: the abilities of decoding, reading comprehension, spelling and writing

Co-articulate: refers to the assimilation of the place of articulation of one speech sound to that of an adjacent speech sound

Correlation: the relationship between two variables

Definitional vocabulary: the bank of words for which meanings are understood

Developmental domains: physical, social, emotional, cognitive and language domains that are essential to children's growth and development

Dialogic reading: process of incorporating conversation as an oral technique in teaching reading skills – based on the research of Grover Whitehurst, et al. (1994)

Direct instruction: teacher-led lesson implementation that is a planned way to introduce, guide and support children's learning of information and skills

Distancing: a questioning technique that personally connects the listener to feelings and events being discussed

Early literacy skills: refers to both precursor skills and the conventional literacy skills of preschool and kindergarten children

Emergent literacy: skills that are recognized as precursors to more conventional forms of reading and writing

Environmental print: product or company name for common product or establishment (e.g., "Coke," "McDonald's")

Expanding language: expand on a child's simple word

Expressive vocabulary: words used for speaking and writing

Grammar: the standard organizational rules governing language

Guided practice: an opportunity for each student to demonstrate grasp of new learning through an activity or exercise under the teacher's direct supervision

High-frequency words: words that appear most often in printed material

Independent practice: a process that gives a student an opportunity to practice a skill independently

Inservice professional development: training that occurs with the purpose of improving skills and knowledge after employees are already engaged as practitioners of their profession

Interactive shared reading: a reading strategy where the adult involves a child or small group of children in reading a book that introduces conventions of print and new vocabulary, or encourages predictions, rhyming, discussion of pictures, and other interactive experiences

Interventions: the instructional practices, methods, strategies, approaches, and programs used by educators and parents to mediate learning

Linguistic complexity: the size of sound units which children are taught

Listening comprehension: the ability to understand what is spoken or read aloud

Modeling: an instructional strategy of demonstrating "the behaviors, skills, and competencies that students are to learn"

Narrative talk: the practice in which children and adults engage in conversations

Onset: the beginning consonant sound in a syllable that precedes the vowel; **b**-ook, **st**-ack, **pl**-ay**m**-ate

Oral language: ability to produce, comprehend, or both, aspects of spoken language

Parallel talk: practice in which an adult (most likely a parent) verbally directs comments to his/her child regarding the child's current activities (e.g., "You are trying to reach your toes, aren't you?" "Look at the big, brown bear you are holding!" "I see you smiling at mommy.")

Phoneme: a minimal sound unit of speech that, when contrasted with another phoneme, affects the meaning of words in a language, as /b/ in *book* contrasts with /t/ in *took*, /k/ in *cook*, and /h/ in *hook*

Phonics: a method of instruction focused on teaching the relationship between the sounds in spoken words and their associated symbols in print

Phonological awareness: the ability to hear and manipulate the separate sounds within words

Phonological short term memory: ability to remember spoken information for a short period of time

Preservice professional development: training that occurs before employees are engaged as practitioners of their profession, often occurring as part of a certificate or degree program

Print awareness: tasks combining elements of alphabet knowledge, concepts about print, and early decoding

Providing feedback: a technique teachers can use to share information with a child about his performance

Reading readiness: combinations of children's understanding of aspects of alphabet knowledge, concepts of print, vocabulary, memory and phonological awareness

Recast: repeat a child's words and expand them into a complete sentence

Rapid naming of letters and digits: rapid naming of sequentially repeating random sets of letters, digits, or both

Rapid naming of objects and colors: rapid naming of sequentially repeating random sets of pictures of objects (e.g., "car," "tree," "house," "man") or colors

Receptive vocabulary: words needed for understanding what is heard and read

Research synthesis: a study that objectively and systematically collects, analyzes, and evaluates data from pre-existing studies to determine answers to specified research questions

Rime: the vowel and all that follows it in the syllable; b-**ook**, st-**ack**, pl-**aym**-**ate**

Scaffolding: providing support at a level just above children's current skill level that pushes them to a slightly higher level of skill

Self talk: occurs when an adult describes and labels what he is doing for a child; often used to increase children's familiarity with words and knowledge of word meanings

Shared reading: a reading strategy where the adult involves a child or small group of children in reading a book that may or may not introduce conventions of print and new vocabulary, or encourage predictions, rhyming, discussion of pictures, and other interactive experiences

Syllable: a minimal unit of sequential speech sounds comprised of a vowel sound or a vowel-consonant combination

Syntax: the rules that govern how sentences are organized and the order and relationships of words

Synthesis: putting together as in blending

Systematic, explicit instruction: a program or way of instruction that includes precise directions for teaching specific material in a logical sequence

Visual processing: ability to match or discriminate visually presented symbols

Visual skills: skills required in motor tasks such as copying or drawing or in memory tasks such as recalling visually-presented information

Writing or writing name: ability to write letters in isolation on request or write own name

REFERENCES

Arnold, D.H., Lonigan, C.J., Whitehurst, G.J., & Epstein, J.N. (1994). Accelerating language development through picture book reading: Replication and extension to a videotape training format. *Journal of Educational Psychology, 86*(2), 235-243.

Benner, G.J., Trout, A., Nordness, P.D., Nelson, J.R., Epstein, M.H., Knobel, M., Epstein, A., Maguire, K., & Birdsell, R. (2002). The effects of the language for learning program on the receptive language skills of kindergarten children. *Journal of Direct Instruction, 2*(2), 67-74.

Collins III, J.W., & O'Brien, N.P. (Eds.). (2003). *The Greenwood dictionary of education.* Westport, CT: Greenwood Press.

Fleming, D. (1991). *In the tall, tall grass.* New York: Henry Holt and Company.

Girolametto, L., Pearce, P.S., & Weitzman, E. (1996). Interactive focused stimulation for toddlers with expressive vocabulary delays. *Journal of Speech and Hearing Research, 39,* 1274-1283.

Hamilton, M. (1977). Social learning and the transition from babbling to initial words. *The Journal of Genetic Psychology, 130,* 211-220.

Hecht, S.A., & Close, L. (2002). Emergent literacy skills and training time uniquely predict variability in responses to phonemic awareness training in disadvantaged kindergartners. *Journal of Experimental Child Psychology, 82*(2), 93-115.

High, P.C., LaGasse, L., Becker, S., Ahlgren, I., & Gardner, A. (2000). Literacy promotion in primary care pediatrics: Can we make a difference? *Pediatrics, 105*(4), 927-934.

Lonigan, C.J., Driscoll, K., Phillips, B.M., Cantor, B.G., Anthony, J.L. & Goldstein, H. (2003). A Computer-Assisted Instruction Phonological Sensitivity Program for Preschool Children At-Risk for Reading Problems. *Journal of Early Intervention, 25*(4), 248.

McGee, L.M., & Ukrainetz, T.A. (2009). Using scaffolding to teach phonemic awareness in preschool and kindergarten. *Reading Teacher, 62, 599-603.*

Mioduser, D., Tur-Kaspa, H., & Leitner, I. (2000). The learning value of computer-based instruction of early reading skills. *Journal of Computer Assisted Learning, 16,* 54-63.

Morrow, L.M., O'Connor, E.M., & Smith, J.K. (1990). Effects of a story reading program on the literacy development of at-risk kindergarten children. *Journal of Reading Behavior, 22*(3), 255-275.

National Early Literacy Panel. (2008). *Developing early literacy: Report of the National Early Literacy Panel.* Washington, DC: National Institute for Literacy.

Phillips, B.M., Clancy-Menchetti, J., & Lonigan, C.J. (2008). Successful phonological awareness instruction with preschool children: Lessons from the classroom. *Topics in Early Childhood Special Education, 28*(1), 3-17.

Robertson, S.B., & Weismer, S.E. (1999). Effects of treatment on linguistic and social skills in toddlers with delayed language development. *Journal of Speech, Language, and Hearing Research, 42*, 1234-1248.

Scarborough, H.S., & Dobrich, W. (1994). On the efficacy of reading to preschoolers. *Developmental Review, 14*, 245-302.

Senechal, M. (2006*).* The Effect of Family Literacy Interventions On Children's Acquisition of Reading From Kindergarten to Grade 3. A Meta-Analytic Review. Washington, DC: National Institute for Literacy.

Smith, C., & Fluck, M. (2000). (Re-) Constructing pre-linguistic interpersonal processes to promote language development in young children with deviant or delayed communication skills. *British Journal of Educational Psychology, 70*, 369-389.

Strickland, D. & Schickedanz, J. (2004). *Learning about print in preschool: Working with letters, words, and beginning links with phonemic awareness.* Newark, DE: International Reading Association.

Valdez-Menchaca, M.C., & Whitehurst, G.J. (1992). Accelerating language development through picture book reading: A systematic extension to Mexican day care. *Developmental Psychology, 28*(6), 1106-1114.

Wasik, B.A., & Bond, M.A. (2001). Beyond the pages of a book: Interactive book reading and language development in preschool classrooms. *Journal of Educational Psychology, 93*(2), 243-250.

Whitehurst, G.J., Falco, F.L., Lonigan, C.J., Fischel, J.E., DeBaryshe, B.D., Valdez-Menchaca, M.C., & Caulfield, M. (1988). Accelerating language development through picture book reading. *Developmental Psychology, 24*(4), 552-559.

National Center for Families Learning
Louisville, KY
www.familieslearning.org

www.ingramcontent.com/pod-product-compliance
Lightning Source LLC
Chambersburg PA
CBHW081539040426

42447CB00014B/3427